ANIMAL IDIOMS

Lazy as a Dog: Are Dogs Sluggish?

BY MARNE VENTURA

CONTENT CONSULTANT
SARAH-ELIZABETH BYOSIERE, PhD
DIRECTOR OF THE THINKING DOG CENTER
ASSISTANT PROFESSOR
HUNTER COLLEGE

Kids Core
An Imprint of Abdo Publishing
abdobooks.com

abdobooks.com

Published by Abdo Publishing, a division of ABDO, PO Box 398166, Minneapolis, Minnesota 55439. Copyright © 2022 by Abdo Consulting Group, Inc. International copyrights reserved in all countries. No part of this book may be reproduced in any form without written permission from the publisher. Kids Core™ is a trademark and logo of Abdo Publishing.

Printed in the United States of America, North Mankato, Minnesota.
102021
012022

THIS BOOK CONTAINS RECYCLED MATERIALS

Cover Photo: Patryk Kosmider/Shutterstock Images
Interior Photos: Olha Tsiplyar/Shutterstock Images, 4–5; Shutterstock Images, 6, 9 (beagle), 15, 24; Ekaterina Brusnika/Shutterstock Images, 8; Eric Iseelee/Shutterstock Images, 9 (terrier), 9 (great dane), 9 (German shepherd), 9 (poodle); Africa Studio/Shutterstock Images, 9 (pug); Irina Oxilixo Danilova/Shutterstock Images, 9 (golden retriever); Monkey Business Images/Shutterstock Images, 11; Patryk Kosmider/Shutterstock Images, 12–13; Angelique van Heertum/Shutterstock Images, 14; Gladskikh Tatiana/Shutterstock Images, 16; Aleksey Boyko/Shutterstock Images, 18; Amit Pansuriya/Shutterstock Images, 20–21; Jose Luis Stephens/Shutterstock Images, 22; Figure 8 Photos/iStockphoto, 26; Yakobchuk Viacheslav/Shutterstock Images, 28 (top); Anurak Pongpatimet/Shutterstock Images, 28 (bottom); Noska Photo/Shutterstock Images, 29 (top); Adam Kaz/iStockphoto, 29 (bottom).

Editor: Christine Ha
Series Designer: Katharine Hale

Library of Congress Control Number: 2021941217

Publisher's Cataloging-in-Publication Data

Names: Ventura, Marne, author.
Title: Lazy as a dog: are dogs sluggish? / by Marne Ventura
Other title: are dogs sluggish?
Description: Minneapolis, Minnesota : Abdo Publishing, 2022 | Series: Animal idioms | Includes online resources and index.
Identifiers: ISBN 9781532196683 (lib. bdg.) | ISBN 9781644946473 (pbk.) | ISBN 9781098218492 (ebook)
Subjects: LCSH: Dogs--Juvenile literature. | Dogs--Behavior--Juvenile literature. | Physical activity--Juvenile literature. | Animal instinct--Juvenile literature. | Idiomatic expressions--Juvenile literature.
Classification: DDC 599.772--dc23

CONTENTS

CHAPTER 1
Taking a Break 4

CHAPTER 2
Are Some Dogs Lazy? 12

CHAPTER 3
Hardworking Dogs 20

Dog Facts 28
Glossary 30
Online Resources 31
Learn More 31
Index 32
About the Author 32

Laptops allow people to do many different things to pass time, such as listening to music or playing games.

Taking a Break

Asa and Talia lay on the living room carpet. Both wore headphones attached to Asa's laptop. Talia was showing Asa a new song by one of her favorite bands.

Dog owners often pick dogs that match their lifestyles. For example, active people will often pick energetic dogs they can run and play with.

Dad came down the stairs. "Why aren't the kids outside playing?" he asked. "It's the first day of summer vacation!"

Mom laughed. "They both seem lazy as dogs," she said. "But I think they need a break after a busy year of school!"

What Are Idioms?

Lazy as a dog is an idiom. An idiom is a phrase that is often used in a certain language. It usually means something other than the words that make up the idiom. *Lazy as a dog* describes a person who doesn't seem to want to work or play. Like dogs lying on the floor, Asa and Talia seem to be spending their time resting or doing nothing. But are dogs really sluggish?

Dogs come in all shapes, colors, and sizes.

There are more than 400 breeds of dogs in the world. They are divided into groups based on their behavior, size, and appearance. Most dogs will spend about half the day sleeping. But every breed is different. Even within a breed, dogs' behavior can vary a lot. Some dogs are happy lying around most of the day. Others are happiest when they are working or playing.

Dog Breed Groups

Hound group bred to pursue warm-blooded game

Working group developed to assist humans in various jobs

Terrier group bred to deal with rodents and other vermin

Toy group small dogs bred for companionship

Herding group developed for moving livestock

Non-Sporting group bred for jobs that don't fit well into the other groups

Sporting group bred to assist hunters in the capture of feathered game

The American Kennel Club divides dog breeds into seven groups. The groups are based on the kind of work that each breed does best. One dog from each group is shown in the graphic above.

Dogs and Humans

Scientists estimate that humans and dogs have lived side-by-side for about 14,000 years. Dogs have long helped people with work such as hunting or herding. Later, people learned that mating two dogs who were good at certain tasks produced offspring who were also good at those jobs. This is called breeding.

Dogs play an important role in human society. Many families keep dogs as pets. Some working dogs help the military and the police. Others serve as eyes or ears for people with disabilities. Although dogs need a lot of rest, it is often well deserved. Throughout history, dogs have gained a reputation for being loyal friends and hard workers.

Many humans consider their pet dogs a part of their family.

Explore Online

Visit the website below. Does it give any new information about dogs that was not in Chapter One?

Domestic Dogs
abdocorelibrary.com/lazy-as-a-dog

Though some dogs have lower energy than others, all dogs still need exercise and activity to stay healthy and happy.

CHAPTER **2**

Are Some Dogs Lazy?

Each dog is different. Breeds vary in energy. Dogs within each breed can differ too. Like humans, each dog is unique and has its own personality.

Dog agility is a sport where dogs are trained to complete obstacle courses.

Some dogs are **motivated** and busy. Others spend much of their time resting. Some dogs are taught to be calm so they are easier to care for. For example, high energy dogs have active minds. They were originally bred to do jobs with lots of activity. Owners can help calm them down with exercise and sports. They can also try putting their dogs' minds to work with puzzles and other thinking games.

Some owners take their active dogs to play in the water to help burn off some energy.

Dogs are good at picking up on human emotions and will respond based on how they believe their owners are feeling.

Dog Intelligence

Some dogs are quite smart. Scientists report that an average dog's **intelligence** is about the same as a two- to two-and-a-half-year-old human toddler. Dogs also have a lot of social intelligence. Dogs are good at reading human behavior and paying attention to how humans communicate with each other.

In one study, dogs watched their owners be given two boxes. The dog did not know the contents of either box. The owner would act positively toward one and negatively toward the other. The dogs went to the positive box 81 percent of the time. This showed that dogs can pick up and respond to humans' judgment and behavior.

How Wolves Became Dogs

Dogs and wolves are **descendants** of the same wild wolflike ancestor. Some scientists believe humans began to tame and breed wolves up to 30,000 years ago. Others think that wolves just started following human camps. Wolves that were more likely to stay near human camps had access to more food. They ate hunters' leftover scraps. These wolves survived and lived alongside humans.

Many pet owners enjoy teaching their dogs simple tricks like a high five or sit.

Scientists also report that the average dog can learn about 165 words. Some dogs can even count and understand basic math. Other dogs are great at tricking other dogs or people to get rewards, like treats. Many dogs can also solve complex problems. One professor taught a dog the names of 1,022 toys. When he told the dog to pick up a certain toy, the dog got the right one 95 percent of the time.

Primary Source

In a study, researchers raised wolf pups with much more human contact than dog puppies. Even so, the wolves hid from unknown people. The dogs ran up to the people. Researcher Hannah Salomons said:

> Dogs are born with this . . . ability to understand that we're communicating with them and we're trying to cooperate with them.

Source: Robin A. Smith. "You Can Snuggle Wolf Pups All You Want." *Duke Today*, 12 July 2021, today.duke.edu. Accessed 8 Sept. 2021.

What's the Big Idea?

Read this quote carefully. What is its main idea? Explain how the main idea is supported by details.

Military and police dogs often wear protective gear while working.

CHAPTER 3

Hardworking Dogs

Historians have evidence of dogs helping people during wartime since 600 BC. In 2019, there were about 1,600 working dogs in the US Department of Defense. Dogs serve in the military in many ways. They sniff out bombs, stand guard, and even skydive!

Service dogs can help people with disabilities by doing daily tasks such as opening doors.

Dogs are well suited for these jobs. Their sense of smell is 10,000 times better than any military device. Military dogs learn how to do these tasks from skilled **trainers**.

Service Dogs

Service dogs go through special training to help people with disabilities. Golden retrievers, Labrador retrievers, and German shepherds are often service dogs. They assist people with **impaired** hearing, vision, and mobility in their daily lives. For example, they can help people pick up items or cross the street safely.

Service dogs can also recognize health issues, such as seizures or heart attacks. They can get help. These dogs also give people with disabilities self-confidence and independence. For example, Thomas Panek is a marathon runner who lost his vision in his early twenties. In 2019, his three Labrador retriever guide dogs took turns helping him run the 13.1-mile (21-km) New York City Half Marathon. They finished the run in 2 hours, 20 minutes, and 51 seconds.

Some police dogs work at the airport. They are trained to sniff out dangerous items that may be hidden in luggage.

K9 Units and Search & Rescue Dogs

Police dogs are trained to protect their human coworkers, chase and hold suspected criminals, and sniff out illegal items. Henny is a black Labrador retriever who served the Seattle Fire Department for six years as a K9 arson dog. He helped the fire department by sniffing out petroleum, a liquid that can cause dangerous fires or explosions. Henny was a part of 134 investigations. He helped people make arrests for illegal fires and figure out why certain fires occurred.

Dog Jobs

Dogs have helped hunters and farmers for hundreds of years. Watchdogs have been around for a long time too. People in modern times use dogs' super sense of smell for new jobs. Dogs can sniff out cancer, track whales, and protect museum art by detecting harmful insects.

Dogs can sniff out people trapped under piles of snow, dirt, or rocks.

Search and rescue dogs help emergency service workers. Search teams train breeds such as Border collies and Labrador retrievers to use their sense of smell to find missing people. The dogs train from six months to two years. Search and rescue dogs can search for eight hours straight in all kinds of **terrain**, day or night.

So, is the idiom *lazy as a dog* true? The answer is no. Different breeds and individuals have various energy levels. When they're not active, they will rest or sleep. But most dogs are eager to play with their owners and work with their trainers to do their jobs. When asked to do a job, they work hard to get it done. For thousands of years, dogs have been loyal companions and helpers to humans.

Further Evidence

Look at the website below. Does it give any new evidence to support Chapter Three?

Can Canines Have Careers?

abdocorelibrary.com/lazy-as-a-dog

Dog Facts

Dogs have lived and worked alongside humans for thousands of years.

High-energy working dogs sniff out bombs and other dangerous items for the military.

Police dogs and search and rescue dogs help during emergency situations.

Service dogs give people with disabilities self-confidence and independence.

Glossary

descendant
a person or animal that comes from a specific ancestor that existed at an earlier time

impaired
having a disability of some kind; unable to function at full strength or ability

intelligence
the ability to apply knowledge and skills

motivated
eager to do something

terrain
a type of land, such as rocky or marshy

trainers
people who teach dogs behaviors and skills

Online Resources

To learn more about dogs, visit our free resource websites below.

Visit **abdocorelibrary.com** or scan this QR code for free Common Core resources for teachers and students, including vetted activities, multimedia, and booklinks, for deeper subject comprehension.

Visit **abdobooklinks.com** or scan this QR code for free additional online weblinks for further learning. These links are routinely monitored and updated to provide the most current information available.

Learn More

Holmes, Parker. *K9 and Military Dogs*. Abdo, 2019.

Lajiness, Katie. *Labrador Retrievers*. Abdo, 2018.

Quattlebaum, Mary. *Hero Dogs*. National Geographic, 2017.

Index

American Kennel Club, 9

Border collies, 26

German shepherds, 9, 22
Golden retrievers, 9, 22, 25

idioms, 7, 27
intelligence, 16–18

K9 units, 24–25

Labrador retrievers, 22, 23, 25, 26

Panek, Thomas, 23

Salomons, Hannah, 19
search and rescue dogs, 26
service dogs, 22–23

training, 22, 24, 26, 27

US Department of Defense, 21

wolves, 17, 19

About the Author

Marne Ventura is the author of more than 100 books for children. A former elementary school teacher, she holds a Master's in Education from the University of California. Marne and her husband live in California.